Montreal's

BEST *TERRASSES*

Dining

Montreal's BEST *TERRASSES* Dining

Joanna Fox

Véhicule Press

Véhicule Press acknowledges the support of the Government of Canada's Book Industry Development Program

Cover design: David Drummond
Inside imaging: Simon Garamond
Printing: Marquis Book Printing Inc.

CATALOGUING IN PUBLICATION DATA

Fox, Joanna, 1980-
Montreal's best terrasses dining, 2012-2013 / Joanna Fox.
Includes index.

ISBN: 978-1-55065-317-5

1. Restaurants—Québec (Province)—Montréal—Guidebooks.
2. Montréal (Québec)—Guidebooks. I. Title.

TX907.5.C22 M6 2012 647.95714'28 C2011-901222-7

Published by Véhicule Press

514.844.6073 FAX 514.844.7543

www.vehiculepress.com

CANADIAN DISTRIBUTION
LitDistCo
www.litdistco.ca
800-591-6250

U.S. DISTRIBUTION
Independent Publishers Group, Chicago, Illinois
www.ipgbook.com
800-888-4741

Printed in Canada on FSC certified paper.

To my parents, Pat and Bill Fox,
for their constant dining enthusiasm,
support and love.

Contents

Acknowledgements

Thank you to everyone who was involved in this guide—from your suggestions to your dining company, this book would never have been completed without you. To all my friends who were dragged along all over the city—I owe you dinner.

Introduction

Montreal is a food lover's city. From little known hole-in-the wall diners to upscale, media blitzed restaurants, specialty stores to open-air markets, we are continuously spoiled for quality and choice. If there is one thing Montrealers love more than eating out it is eating outside. As soon as the glimmer of spring sunshine comes out, so do we, in droves. Starved for the warm sunlight on our pale, weary, winter skin, we will dine outside until it's time for hats and gloves. The way we see it, if we made it through the winter, we deserve to be outside as much as humanly possible, all summer long. This past year has been an outdoor dining explosion with many restaurants setting up tables and chairs on the sidewalk in front of their establishments to maximize the outdoor potential. There has also been a restaurant boom and having a *terrasse* or backyard-dining area seems to be on the top of everyone's list of must-haves. This guide barely scratches the surface of what Montreal has to offer, but it's a compilation of what I consider to be the best choices in the city, taking into account atmosphere, quality and price. I hope you enjoy these restaurant experiences as much as I did.

Alphabetical List of Restaurants

Aux Vivres

Originally a cozy little vegan and vegetarian restaurant that popped up on St-Dominique in 1997, Aux Vivres moved in 2005 to a more spacious location on St-Laurent that boasts a lovely *terrasse* out back. Stemming from the idea that healthy vegan and vegetarian cuisine does not have to be bland and boring, Aux Vivres prides itself on high quality and flavorful dishes. Respected among vegetarians and non-vegetarians alike, they favor local produce and create seasonal dishes that span a variety of cuisines. The atmosphere at Aux Vivres is friendly and relaxed and the sheltered *terrasse* at the back is a cool shaded spot for lunch or dinner. Some of the dishes I like to start with are the dhal soup or their homemade chapattis served with vegetarian butter. What's so perfect about Aux Vivres is that not only is the food great, but you really do feel good eating it. The Dragon bowl is always a favorite—a mixture of shredded vegetables, lettuce, sprouts, toasted sesame seeds and their special dragon sauce, served with brown rice. The BLT made with coconut bacon is also surprisingly tasty and passes the carnivore test. There are also salads, sandwiches, burgers, smoothies, juices and desserts; all proving that healthy food does indeed make you happy.

4631 St-Laurent
514.842.3479
Metro/Bus: Mont Royal, then bus 97 west, or bus 11
Web: www.auxvivres.com
Hours: 11am-11pm daily
Cards: V, MC, Interac
Wheelchair access: steps
Average meal: $15

Banquise, La

La Banquise is a Montreal icon and a mecca for poutine. Located just down the street from Lafontaine Park, this 24-hour diner offers an extensive poutine selection, great Quebec greasy spoon specials like burgers and hot dogs, a young, vibrant atmosphere, and a fabulous trellised *terrasse*, with tables under parasols out back. Whether it's for a quick lunch, or a late night dinner, this place is consistently hopping around the clock. When the bars let out at 3am, young people swarm to this place to gather and graze. Its colorful décor and casual setting match the resto's attitude and the food they serve. The classic poutine is always a good choice, but if you fancy something Tex-Mex you might want to try the Taquise, with guacamole, sour cream and tomatoes. A personal favorite is the T-Rex with ground beef, pepperoni, bacon and sausage—a real show stopper. There is also a vegetarian poutine option, sandwiches, salads and daily specials. La Banquise also supports local industry and serves Quebec micro-brewery beers. If you're in the neighborhood early enough to check it out, there is also a Banquise breakfast menu. With great staff that always seems to be having as much fun working as the diners are eating, it's hard to go wrong here for a true Montreal experience.

994 Rachel est
514.525.2415
Metro/Bus: Mont Royal
Web: restolabanquise.com
Hours: 24 hours daily
Cards: cash, Interac
Wheelchair access: stairs
Average meal: $12

Bice

If you're looking to dine *al fresco* and love modern Italian cuisine, Bice just might be your next *terrasse* choice. With its gorgeous 250-seat outdoor *terrasse* right in the heart of downtown Montreal, this is a popular gathering spot for those with good taste and deep pockets. The restaurant itself is sleek, stylish and modern, and extends the same approach to their celebrated outdoor dining area. Covered in a white canvas tent and shaded from Sherbrooke Street by flowers, trellises and foliage, when this place is full, it's not hard to imagine that you are at a fashion party or gallery launch. For those who are lovers of all things Italian, this menu will make you weak in the knees. Using only the best produce, the quality of food is exceptional, as is their Italian wine list. For a simple salad to start, it's hard to go wrong with the freshness of the mozzarella di bufala, vine-ripe tomatoes, olives and prosciutto, or the grilled octopus, navy bean purée, cherry tomatoes, green olives, pickled red onion and pulled foccacia. If you're truly in the mood for a long, lazy Italian meal, I suggest a pasta course next, followed by a meat or fish dish. The spaghetti with lobster, tomatoes, garlic, chilies and zucchini flowers is very seductive, but it's also hard to pass up the taglioni with braised veal cheeks, mushrooms, rapini and aged pecorino. The veal chop Milanese is one of their main course specialties, and the fish of the day is always an appropriate seasonal bet. Whether it's a special occasion or simply a celebration of summertime, Ristorante Bice is truly a special experience.

1504 Sherbrooke ouest
514.937.6009
Metro/Bus: Guy-Concordia
Web: bicemontreal.com
Hours: Mon.-Sat.: 6pm-11pm; Sunday 6pm-10pm
Cards: all major
Wheelchair access: no
Average main: $40

Bofinger – NDG

A few years ago the Southern BBQ craze rippled through the entire Montreal restaurant scene, with pulled pork, smoked ribs and fried chicken turning up on every menu from high-end dining to low-end dives. One of the first places to start pulling, smoking and spicing up our menus was the original (and I think the best) Bofinger—on Sherbrooke Street West in the borough of Notre-Dame-de-Grace. With checkered tablecloths set atop picnic tables, the atmosphere at Bofinger screams Southern hospitality. In the summer, they set up tables out front where you can enjoy finger-lickin' good food at really reasonable prices—the way BBQ food is supposed to be eaten. They truly pride themselves on their smoked meats which they dry rub and smoke with maple wood for up to 24 hours. The menu is straightforward—you choose your meat or combination of meats; pick one of the 6 choices of BBQ sauces (I prefer the classic Texas) and a side such as potato salad, baked beans or mac n' cheese. If you're not in the mood for chicken or ribs, there are pulled pork and brisket sandwiches, burgers, poutine and chicken wings. Bofinger isn't fancy and it doesn't have table service, but the food is good, it's a fun atmosphere and it's a great place for families to enjoy a BBQ minus the mess.

5667 Sherbrooke ouest
514.315.5056
Metro/Bus: Vendome and bus 105
Web: www.bofinger.ca
Hours: 11am-11pm daily
Cards: V, MC
Wheelchair access: no
Average meal: $15

Boris Bistro

Old Montreal is a perfect setting for eating outside, but unfortunately, like many areas geared towards the tourist industry, there are a lot of over-priced mediocre restaurants preying on visitors who flock to this part of town in the summer. Boris Bistro, although not overlooking the scenic port, is a very large, popular *terrasse* that opens up right onto McGill College in the heart of Old Montreal. A hot ticket for lunching locals, this is also a great spot for a 5-à-7 drink and some light after-work nibbles before dinner. The front of Boris Bistro is the stone façade of a classic Montreal building , giving way to tables under umbrellas, plants, flowers and an overall sense that this is the swankiest overgrown garden you've ever been in. The food here lingers between French bistro and Italian trattoria, with entrées like an endive, beet, walnut and blue cheese salad, caponata on mild goat cheese with tomato coulis and virgin olive oil, foie gras, or a charcuterie plate. Something that can't be missed is their fries cooked in duck fat. If you've never tried this before, do yourself a favor and forever ruin eating fries any other way. For mains, there are some lighter options like the Mediterranean chicken salad, salmon or beef tartare, as well as pastas, risotto, duck and even grilled buffalo. Boris Bistro's food is well priced for quality and is a wonderful *terrasse* spot for an Old Montreal meal option.

465 McGill
514.848.9575
Metro/Bus: Square Victoria
Web: borisbistro.com
Hours: Mon.-Fri.: 11:30am-11pm; Sat.-Sun.: noon-11pm
Cards: all major, Interac
Wheelchair access: yes
Average main: $20

Bottega Pizzeria

If you're looking for a true Little Italy experience, Bottega is as good as they come. The owners actually brought in Italians from Naples to build their pizza oven for them. The pizza here is something different from the paper-thin crust many places have built their reputation on. Bottega's dough is springy and the crust quite thick. The center is softer and floppier than you may be used to, sending you to your knife and fork, but the flavor is all there. This is a real summer dinner hotspot and reservations are a must. Like many places in Little Italy, Bottega places several tables outside on the sidewalk under their awning where the people-watching is almost as good as the food. With a team of affable (and very good-looking) staff, service is quick and efficient. If you're not in the mood for pizza, Bottega has a nice variety of salads and entrées that you can mix and match to make your meal. There are also seasonal nightly specials that are always a good bet since they only use only the highest quality, freshest ingredients. Their wine list is above average and offers plenty of choice to quench your thirst. Another great bonus of dining in Little Italy is that the coffee at the end of the meal is excellent and you will definitely need a little espresso shot before you head out. (Bottega has now opened a branch in Laval: 2059 St-Martin West, 450.688.1100.)

65 St-Zotique est
514.277.8104
Metro/Bus: Beaubien, then 18 bus; or St-Laurent metro, then bus 55
Web: www.bottega.ca
Hours: Tues.-Sun.: 5pm-midnight
Cards: all major
Wheelchair access:
Average main: $18

Boucan, Le

Summertime is the perfect season to indulge in an all-time favorite classic—BBQ. A recent food trend and worthy contender against high-end mac n' cheese with its undeniable comfort appeal, the BBQ craze has been popping up all over the city, softening higher end menus with pulled pork sandwiches and house-smoked ribs. Whether or not this Southern-style food will stick around in this not-so-Southern climate is up for debate, but Le Boucan, is a fairly new restaurant specializing in BBQ done right—the smoker is visible through their semi-open kitchen. With a little *terrasse* in the back, it's a great outdoor dining option. Situated in the now resto-populated district of Little Burgundy, this joint is run by a trio of committed BBQ enthusiasts. If you got on that mac n' cheese bandwagon, you can have a pretty good version here, but if it's too hot for a heaping serving of pasta and gooey cheese, go for the house-smoked specialties. I recommend the pulled pork, the chicken or the ribs. If you can't decide on just one, try the "Pit Boss" platter for sharing. Although meant for two, don't be shy to share between more, it's a massive plate of food with the aforementioned meats, coleslaw and potato salad. So if it's BBQ that you crave and you want to enjoy the summer night outside, check out Le Boucan for a hearty, smoky meal.

1886 Notre-Dame ouest
514.439.4555
Metro/Bus: Georges-Vanier
Web: www.leboucan.com
Hours: Tues.-Wed., Sun.: noon-11:30pm;
Thurs.-Sat.: noon-11pm; closed Mon.
Cards: all major
Wheelchair access: steps
Average main: $18

Boustan

Crescent Street is a well-known downtown Montreal strip for busy business lunches and rowdy late nights. A tourist hotspot, especially during the summer and during the Montreal Grand-Prix, this three-block area is always hopping. There are a handful of obvious places to drink and eat outside, but ask any Montrealer where to get the most bang for your buck and they'll tell you it's Boustan. A tiny Lebanese restaurant where you order and get your food at the counter, in the summer they set up tables outside so you can enjoy the buzz on the street. This business has been serving affordable, delicious food for as long as I have been of legal drinking age and has become quite a rendezvous for late night eats after the bars close. With an array of combo plates and pitas, the juicy meat selections are slowly rotating on spits, which they shave off right in front of you. The chicken shawarma is one of the best in the city, topped with your choice of beets, eggplant, cauliflower, pickeled turnip, hummus and garlic sauce, then grilled to toasted perfection. The beef shawarma is seasoned nicely and their falafels will convert any meat eater. At Boustan, there is always something for every appetite and taste. Open for lunch, dinner, and until 4am, if you're craving some excellent Middle Eastern cuisine, Boustan will not disappoint.

2020A Crescent
514.843.3576
Metro/Bus: Guy-Concordia
Web: www.boustan.ca
Hours: Mon.-Sat.: 11am-4am; Sun: 5pm-4am
Cards: V, MC, Interac
Wheelchair access: stairs
Average meal: $10

Brasserie Reservoir

Reservoir may be one of the Plateau's best lunch/brunch spots if you're looking for an above-average dining experience. Slightly more expensive than some places in the area, you definitely get beyond what you pay for at this impeccably-designed microbrewery and brasserie. In the summer, they open up their second floor *terrasse*, as well as the sliding windows on the main floor, bringing the dining room right onto Duluth Street. There is no better seat in the house than overlooking from above this busy little street corner. The menu changes daily and there is a nice selection of vegetarian, seafood and meat dishes, all seasonal and local when possible. And what better way to wash down the meal than with one of their many homemade beers, ranging from white and pale ales to stouts—some of the best in the city. For brunch specialties there are gravlax, crepes or the veal liver; for lunch their soups of the day, tartares and fish and chips are always good. If you can't make it there for lunch or weekend brunch, there is also an evening snack menu—octopus, coco beans and chorizo, grilled cheese with Gruyère, caramelized tomatoes and cucumber pickle, or cod fritters with lemon mayonnaise. Whether it's just for a pint and a small snack, or for a longer, lazy lunch with wine, Brasserie Reservoir is a great summer choice.

9 Duluth est
514.849.7779
Metro/Bus: Sherbrooke, or 55 bus
Web: www.brasseriereservoir.ca
Summer hours: Daily 3pm-1am-; until 3am later in the week (Kitchen open 5pm-11pm)
Cards: all major
Wheelchair access: not terrace
Average main: $17

Bremner, Le

The name Chuck Hughes is well known in Montreal, not only for his Old Montreal restaurant, Garde Manger, but also for his Food Network television show Chuck's Day Off. With his handsome boyish grin and his numerous tattoos, and his passion for everything from crab and oysters to durian fruit, there's no denying Hughes loves food. Last summer he opened his second restaurant, Le Bremner, also in Old Montreal. More laid back than Garde Manger, Le Bremner celebrates Hughes' love of seafood such as scallops on the half shell, as well as some of his comfort food favorites. Located on St-Paul East, blink and you might miss the small staircase off the street that leads into the unmarked doorway that is Bremner. You might also never notice that through the back door of the restaurant is another set of steps that lead up to a sheltered outdoor dining area complete with its own seafood bar and ceiling fans for those hot summer nights. Surrounded by stone, this *terrasse* feels more grotto than garden and is a nice private shelter from the bustling Old Montreal streets. With a menu designed for sharing, you might want to order lobster toast au gratin, seared tuna foccaccia or the spicy honey bread with rosemary and ricotta before moving on to the mains. From the stovetop and broiler Le Bremner offers delicious choices such as skate with garlic potatoes, fried pork cutlet with bok choy, spaghetti squash and meatballs, and trout with a classic Bearnaise sauce. Next time you are in Old Montreal, treat yourself to the Chuck Hughes experience

361 St-Paul est
514.544.0446
Metro/Bus: Champ-de-mars
Web: www.crownsalts.com
Hours: Mon.-Sat.: 6pm-11:30pm (Kitchen closes at 11.)
Cards: all major
Wheelchair access:
Average meal: $40

Burgundy Lion

The gentrification of Little Burgundy over the past five years has meant that there are now a lot more options for diners, not only in the area, but particularly Notre-Dame street West, which has now become a destination for food lovers. If you're looking for something casual with a gastro-pub British vibe, look no further than the Burgundy Lion. A popular bar for after-work dinner and drinks, The Burgundy Lion has created a polished pub atmosphere with great food, occasional live music and typical British pub activities like broadcasting soccer matches and quiz nights. It's a great spot to sit out on one of their two *terrasses*, relax and indulge in British-inspired pub fare. Once the weather gets warm, they construct a *terrasse* right outside the pub on the sidewalk. If you're looking for something a bit more private or shaded from the sun, there is an intimate and quiet inner courtyard in the center of the bar. Some of their specialties include fun dishes like The London Tea Party (crustless cucumber and tuna sandwiches), their version of a Ploughman's lunch (cold pork pie with cheese fruits and crusty bread), or the Welshman's Bride (Guinness-braised lamb shanks). There are also staples such as their famous fish and chips, bangers and mash, Manchester curry or Burgundy roast. Burgundy Lion offers a dining experience unlike any in the city, with a staff that is always friendly and helpful. If you're a whisky lover, there is a fantastic selection here to end the meal, or begin the night!

2496 Notre-Dame ouest
514.934.0888
Metro/Bus: Lionel-Groulx
Web: www.burgundylion.com
Hours: Mon.-Fri.:11:30am-3am; Sat.-Sun.: 9am-3am
Cards: V, MC, Interac
Wheelchair access: yes
Average main: $20

Buvette Chez Simone

If you're looking for the place where the cool, young, good-looking 20- to 30-somethings hang out for drinks and dinner in the Mile End, Buvette Chez Simone is at the top of the list. Designed with a real eye for style, this narrow bar/restaurant is located on Parc Avenue, just above Villeneuve and is a huge contributor to the re-commercialization of the once rather dismal Parc Avenue. With a horseshoe-shaped bar in the center, plenty of counter seats and tables lining each wall, Buvette is a real hotspot for the 5-à-7 crowd. In the summer, they have a lovely front *terrasse* where you can hang out, drink, and sample their light dinner fare. In addition to house cured charcuterie plates, salads, olives, nuts and nibbles, Buvette also offers a pretty mean roast chicken served on a cutting board and designed to share family-style. With a full bar and a well-selected wine list with specialty imports and an ever-changing selection of wines by the glass, you can always find something you'll like within your price range. Buvette doesn't take reservations so you have to be prepared to wait in line, but for the atmosphere and the hip young energy, it's worth it. A drink at Buvette tends to turn into a bottle, a snack into a full meal and a quick stop before you go out into an evening of fun. It's not to be missed!

4869 Parc
514.750.6577
Metro/Bus: Laurier then bus 51; or bus 80
Web: www.buvettechezsimone.com
Hours: 5pm-midnight daily
Cards: V, MC
Wheelchair access: no
Average meal: $25

Café Cherrier

Some Montreal restaurants give the impression you've walked into a Paris café. Café Cherrier is one of these places. Established in 1931, it has always been an important cultural meeting place, becoming very popular with the bohemian crowd. With its long wood bar, mirrored walls, tiled floors and waiters wearing ties, this is definitely a chic place to brunch, lunch or seriously dine. It has a large wrap-around *terrasse* on the corner of St-Denis and Cherrier with the added touch of plants and flowers that makes their outdoor space appealing to diners and passersby alike. The menu is classically French and the place is always packed, any season. Some of Café Cherrier's specialties are the French onion or fish soup, various terrines or liver mousses, their salmon and beef tartares and of course, the quintessential classic—bavette steak and fries. If you're in the mood for something simple, I suggest the croque monsieur,—the very French grilled ham and cheese sandwich. With a solid wine list and extensive selection of cheeses to go with an after dinner drink, Café Cherrier is a true *terrasse* bistro experience that's great all day long.

3635 St-Denis
514.843.4308
Metro/Bus: Sherbrooke
Web: www.cafecherrier.ca
Hours: Mon.-Fri.: 7:30am-11pm; Sat.-Sun.: 8:30am-11pm
Cards: all major
Wheelchair access: yes
Average meal: $30

Café de Souvenir and Le Petit Italien

These two restaurants, side by side on Bernard Street in Outremont, are operated by the same owners and have charming little street-front *terrasses* for sitting outside. Café de Souvenir is always a solid breakfast/brunch choice with a menu that goes all day long and a good variety of dishes for every appetite. Under their striped awning, the tightly packed, round bistro tables are reminiscent of a quaint Parisian café. From a croque-monsieur on fresh croissant to a build-your-own egg breakfast, quesadillas, to a darn good hamburger with blue cheese and bacon, there's nothing too fancy or pretentious about this food. If a French café isn't what you're craving, you can stroll right next door for a little taste of Italy. Le Petit Italien is one of my preferred outdoor dining spots—the portions are ample and the prices are reasonable. With all main dishes offered in entrée and main course sizes, this is an ideal spot to eat when all you want is a salad and a small meal. With spaghetti Bolognese that tastes like Nonna's recipe, a seafood risotto and some meat and fish choices, this sleek, polished restaurant is a perfect choice for a hot, hazy summer night. Bernard Street is also a great place to people watch, and after your meal you can stroll down to Bilboquet to get some of the best ice cream in the city.

1261 Bernard Café de Souvenir
514.948.5259
Metro/Bus: Outremont, or by bus take the 80 or 435
Web: cafesouvenir.com
Hours: Mon.-Fri.: 7am-11pm; Sat.-Sun.: 7am-11pm
Cards: V, MC, Interac
Wheelchair access: steps
Average meal: $25

1265 Bernard Le Petit Italien
514.278-0888
Web: lepetititalien.com
Hours: Mon.-Tues.: 5pm-10pm; Wed.: 11:30am-10am;
Thurs.-Fri.: 11:30am-11pm; Sat.-Sun: 5pm-10pm.
Cards: all major, Interac
Wheelchair access: terrasse only
Average meal: $25

Campagnola, La

Convivial Italian restaurants always make me excited to dine out. There is something about a boisterous atmosphere, heaping plates of pasta, a bustling dining room and friendly service that always makes you feel welcome. La Campagnola is definitely one of those places, located in LaSalle and with a great covered summer *terrasse* to boot. Family-run, this restaurant goes the extra mile to make you feel like you've just come over to their house for dinner. With fresh local produce and in-house chacuterie, they often just go from table to table offering a pre-dinner taste of one of their many specialties. Besides the superb Italian food, La Campagnola is also BYOB, which is why it's so popular for parties and family gatherings, not to mention that they have the space to accommodate bigger groups. The menu offers something for everyone, from their take on the Greek salad, to fried calamari, house-made sausages and grilled shrimp. For mains you can try one of their many pasta combinations, as well as chicken, seafood, beef and lamb. Although for some this is a bit off the beaten path, if you want to really work for your meal, you can take a leisurely bike ride along the Lachine Canal and reward yourself at La Campagnola with solid Italian food and a glass of wine.

1708-1714 Dollard, LaSalle
514.363-4066
Metro/Bus: Angrignon, then bus 106
Web: www.lacampagnola.ca
Hours: Tues.-Thurs. & Sunday: 4:30pm-10pm;
Fri.-Sat: 4:30pm-11pm
Cards: all major
Wheelchair access: yes
Average meal: $25

Chilenita, La

This Chilean mini-chain has been making some pretty tasty empanadas for quite some time. With three locations in the Plateau-Mile End district and excellent consistency across the board, La Chilenita definitely deserves a mention. The newest of the three, and the one with an outdoor front *terrasse*, is located on St-Laurent just below St-Viateur. The menu is quite simple and offers specials of the day and plenty of inexpensive meal options. If you're feeling hungry you can never go wrong with the delicious chicken quesadillas, warm and oozing with cheese, salsa and avocados. For something on the lighter side try an empanada, either whole wheat or regular, served with a side of their out-of-this-world hot sauce that I'm tempted to drink. Some of my favorites are the Italian empanada, filled with sausages and spices; the Mediterranean, with eggplant, tomatoes and olives; the spinach and cheese; or the traditional beef with olives. If you're closer to their Marie-Anne and Esplanade location, there is no better place to eat your meal than sitting in Jean-Mance Park, either at one of the many picnic tables, on the grass soaking up the rays, or against a tree in the shade. For a casual meal and a little bit of South American spice, Chilenita is a great summer bet.

5439 St-Laurent (also: 152 Napoleon & 64 Marie-Anne West)
514.277.3030
Metro/Bus: 55 bus
Hours: Mon.: 11:30am-5pm; Tues.-Sat.: 11:30am-9pm
Cards: V,MC, Interac
Wheelchair access: no
Average meal: $10

Club Chasse et Pêche and Le Filet

These two restaurants are owned by the same dynamic and talented team that continues to impress Montrealers with its high level of cuisine and ingredients. Le Club Chasse et Pêche is located in Old Montreal and has one of the city's best outdoor dining areas, reserved for lunchtime dining only. Sit back and enjoy the view of their beautiful garden and be pampered by their professional service and unbeatable seasonal cuisine while sipping wine from a well selected, private-import list. For a slightly younger, more upbeat experience, head on up to Mount Royal Avenue in the Plateau, right in front of Jeanne-Mance Park for some seafood specialties at Le Filet. Although not entirely seafood, this menu does showcase the best of what Quebec has to offer in a minimalist subdued atmosphere. To enjoy a summer night, they've placed tables out in front of the restaurant, a perfect spot overlooking the mountain and the park. Do yourself a favor and try the crab risotto. Whether you're looking for a sylish experience or a nighttime ocean dip, both Le Club Chasse et Pêche and the Filet are an ideal choice!

423 St-Claude Club Chasse et Pêche
514.861.1112
Metro/Bus: Champ-de-mars
Web: www.leclubchasseetpeche.com
Hours: Tues.-Sat.: 6pm-11:30pm
Cards: all major
Wheelchair access: steps
Average meal: $50

219 Mont-Royal ouest Le Filet
514.360-6060
Metro/Bus: Mont-Royal then bus 97 west
Web: www.lefilet.ca
Hours: Tues.-Sat.: 6pm-11:30pm
Cards: all major
Wheelchair access: ramp
Average meal: $35

Cosmos

Some of Montreal's most memorable outdoor eating areas are the most simple. Cosmos, a longtime Montreal breakfast icon and home to an infamous cast of characters, gives us the summer pleasure of expanding their small counter-only seating to a handful of plastic tables and chairs out front on the sidewalk. Not really considered a *terrasse* by any standards, as long as you're sitting outside and enjoying the warm weather, this qualifies as dining *al fresco.* Open daily, you can enjoy some of Cosmos' classic breakfasts, the Mishmash omelet (eggs, bacon, sausage, ham, salami, tomato, onion, cheese with toast) or the Creation sandwich (fried egg, bacon, salami, cheese, lettuce and tomato), or for lunch, you can sink your teeth into one of the best classic diner burgers this city has to offer. Not to mention their potatoes, which will no doubt make you a Cosmos convert for life. But don't expect to have your yoghurt and granola here, this is a heavy duty, hangover curing, loosening-of-the-belt meal that will no doubt fill you up all day long. Very popular in the NDG area, folks flock to this diner from all over the city. As you enjoy your breakfast you can take in the colorful Sherbrooke street atmosphere of this diverse and food-rich neighborhood. Walk off those calories after your meal and check out the amazing Middle Eastern and Korean grocery stores further west down the street that make this strip of NDG a real food lover's find.

5843 Sherbrooke ouest
514.486.3814
Metro/Bus: Vendome, then bus 105
Hours: 7am-5pm daily
Cards: cash only
Wheelchair access: no space
Average meal: $10

Croissanterie Figaro, La

Originally a house in the 1920s, this quaint café on the corner of Hutchinson and Fairmount underwent many transformations—a clothing store, candy store, bakery and fast food restaurant—to arrive at the bustling café it has now become The current owner, Al Charmant, claims that it was the first place in Montreal to have a portable oven. With the oven still there today, Figaro is well known for its very Parisian-style atmosphere and *terrasse,* always packed in the summer and a great place for a light meal. Boasting homemade croissants, this is a relaxing morning stop to quietly sip a coffee and read the newspaper. By midday, it fills up with locals and becomes the perfect spot to get a little sun, sip some wine and have a salad or sandwich. At night it's ideal for a nice meal among the floral ambiance that Figaro has taken so much care in maintaining. The food is casual and fresh and at night there are off-the-menu specials to choose from. If a great ambiance, lovely *terrasse* and excellent food is your fancy, check out this popular Mile End spot.

5200 Hutchison
514.278.6567
Metro/Bus: 80 bus
Web: www.lacroissanteriefigaro.com
Hours: 7am-midnight daily
Cards: all major
Wheelchair access: yes (*terrasse*)
Average meal: $15

Da Emma

There are some places in Montreal that offer an unparalleled dining experience. When people ask me to list some of my favorite restaurants, Da Emma is always at the top of the list. Although not a place for everyday dining, I feel that every Montreal food lover should try to eat here at least once. Part of Da Emma's charm is the cavern-like historic setting in Old Montreal, but it's also the menu, written in Italian, the candle-lit tables, the gorgeous sheltered outdoor patio, and of course, Emma's food. Housed in what was Montreal's first women's prison, Chef Emma heads the kitchen, specializing in Roman cuisine. For a great outdoor setting with quality of food to match, there are few better places to eat in the summertime. Emma's heavenly meatballs in tomato sauce are so delicately held together, you wonder how she manages to keep them in one piece. The pasta with wild mushrooms and olive oil is also a must, as are the lamb dishes, osso bucco and fish. I've never had swordfish cooked like this before—small tender pieces mixed with a cherry tomato sauce and arugula salad—a true gastronomic discovery. With an extensive Italian wine list to match the food, and not to mention the desserts, this is as close to dining in Rome as you're going to get in this city.

777 de la Commune ouest
514.392.1568
Metro/Bus: Square Victoria then bus 61, or by car
Hours: Mon.-Thurs.: noon-10:30pm;
Fri.: noon-11pm; Sat.: 6pm-11:30pm
Cards: all major, no Interac
Wheelchair access: yes
Average main: $40

Dépanneur le Pick Up

Part dépanneur, part restaurant, this original concept was the idea of two ingenious Montrealers who have created a cult following for their casual, daytime, resto-store in Petite Patrie. Making it easier on the staff, you can peruse the fridges yourself and choose your own drinks. Beer? Sure. Cookies? Yep. Cereal, canned goods, popsicles, cat food? Definitely. Convenience aside, Le Dépanneur's food is what has really put them on the map. The pulled pork sandwich—the much-appreciated vegetarian version is also available—is enough to keep you coming back for more. Although the menu is small, there's a great selection of breakfast food and sandwiches, with daily specials. Sitting on one of several picnic tables, either in front or out back, the feeling is a nice mixture of hipster café meets roadside stand, with an overall atmosphere of being away from the city. It is truly a great experience at the Pick-Up, even if occasionally the service tends to be a bit slow when they're really busy. Once a month they have a special dinner night where they invite a local chef to cook a themed meal. If you want to be lucky enough to get a seat, book in advance. It's well worth the wait.

7032 Waverly
514.271.8011
Metro/Bus: de Castelnau, or 55 bus
Web: depanneurlepickup.com
Hours: Mon.-Fri.: 7am-7pm; Sat.: 9am-7pm;
Sun.: 10-6pm
Cards: none
Wheelchair access: one step
Average meal: under $10

Dominion Square Tavern

This Montreal restaurant is currently the coolest place to dine in downtown Montreal, hands down. Located on Metcalfe, just below St-Catherine Street and across from what used to be known as Dominion Square (now Dorchester Square,) this Old-meets-New-World tavern is all class. From the team behind the Plateau bar Baldwin Barmacie and the Mile End's Whisky Café, this polished downtown tavern has black and white tiled floors, warm, subdued lighting, a long wooden bar and a team of extremely good-looking, clean-cut servers who make the experience all the better. Although not a huge terrace, Dominion Square Tavern sets up about half a dozen or so tables out front on the sidewalk (like many Montreal restaurants have now been allowed to do) to accommodate those who want to enjoy the bustling downtown scenery. The best part of Dominion is that it's doesn't just look good, the food meets your expectations and is affordable too. The Ploughman's lunch is their unique take on this traditional British dish with a salmon gravlax or meat option, both accompanied with pickled vegetables, aged cheddar and a deviled egg. Main plates include beef strip loin, mussels, pulled pork sandwich, roasted cod and grilled chicken. For dessert, you can never go wrong with sticky toffee pudding. Open for lunch and dinner, if you are looking for somewhere to eat downtown, you'll be in very good hands at Dominion Square Tavern. Reservations are recommended.

1243 Metcalfe
514.564.5056
Metro/Bus: Peel
Web: www.dominionsquaretavern.com
Hours: Mon.-Fri.: 11:30am-midnight;
Sat.-Sun.:10:30am-midnight
Cards: all major
Wheelchair access: one step
Average meal: $30

Enfants Terribles, Les

Bernard street West in Outremont is hopping in the summer. Everywhere you look there are people eating and drinking at restaurants and *terrasses* in this French-meets-hipster area. One of the newer restaurants on the corner of Champagneur is Les Enfants Terribles. Now a neighborhood favorite, Les Enfants' street-front *terrasse* is the most impressive on the block wrapping around the side to maximize outdoor dining. The front windows of the restaurant also slide open so that you are basically eating outside even if you can't manage to snag a table outside. It's a pretty hot ticket for weekend brunching, but is also great for lunch and dinner any day of the week. With rustic wood accents, chalkboard menus and an open kitchen, this is definitely the most youthful and modern bistro of the Bernard bunch. The menu has a comfort food kind of vibe and includes dishes like Cornish hen, braised lamb shank, bavette and fries, a rib steak for two, burgers, fish and chips, ribs and mac n' cheese. They also have house-smoked salmon, oysters, a nice selection of seafood and a variety of tartares. This is a fantastic people-watching spot, so if you're in the area and want some homey fare, check out Les Enfants Terribles and see why this friendly family-run restaurant is the new golden child.

1257 Bernard ouest
514.759.9918
Metro/Bus: Outremont
Web: www.lesenfantsterriblesbrasserie.ca
Hours: Mon.-Fri.: 11:30am-midnight; Sat.: 9:30am-midnight; Sun.: 9:30am-9pm
Cards: V, MC
Wheelchair access: one step
Average main: $20 (lunch); $30 (supper)

Galanga Bistro Thai

Thai food has always been one of my favorites and Galanga Bistro Thai recently made its way to my top Thai picks here in Montreal. Nestled in the residential part of Outremont along Lajoie Avenue, you can find authentic Thai cuisine at an affordable price with a great outdoor dining area overlooking the picturesque neighborhood. In the former space of Terrasse Justine, Chef Kraisak Kuamsub, who worked at Thailande on Bernard Street, opened up this place with partner Claude Tremblay. Bright and cozy on the inside, the restaurant practically doubles its size with the outdoor space on the sidewalk out front. The name Galanga, also known as galangal, is part of the ginger family and is a common ingredient in many Thai dishes, such as grilled beef salad appetizer, also known as Yum nua nam jim jael—tender morsels of beef combined with cucumber, spring onions, rice, mint and thin shavings of galangal—excellent! On a hot summer night, the green mango salad is also a light refreshing option with matchstick slices of mango, shrimp, coriander, peanuts and lime. For mains my favorite is the green curry with chicken, Thai eggplant, and peppers. Not overly sweet, this dish has pleasant undertones of heat that don't overwhelm the rest of the ingredients and it has a sauce that is great for soaking up with rice. There is also a delicious lamb curry and a flavorful salmon dish worth checking out. With friendly service and a very reasonable wine list, Galanga Bistro Thai is a great *terrasse* option for lovers of Thai food.

1231 Lajoie
438-438-3289
Metro/Bus: Outremont
Tue-Fri: 11:30am-2pm, Tue-Sun: 5-10pm
Cards: all major
Wheelchair access: one step
Average meal: $15-$20

Griffintown Café

If you haven't checked out the Notre-Dame strip west of the downtown core lately, you're definitely missing out on a whole slew of new spots. Revamped apartments, condos, grocery stores, bars, live music and great little eateries, this whole area has been slowly undergoing a gentrification that is giving the Plateau-Mile End some stiff competition. One of the newer kids on the block is the aptly-named Griffintown, an homage to the neighborhood in the Southwest part of the downtown area bordering the canal and originally settled by Irish immigrants in the early 19th century. Once a working-class neighborhood, it is now a breeding ground for new business. Opened in July 2010, Griffintown is a gorgeous space that offers weekend brunch, lunch and dinner, along with live music Tuesday through Saturday. There's also a bonus—a great *terrasse* out back shaded by large parasols and undetectable to the gaze of passersby. With exposed brick walls and incredibly high ceilings flooded with natural light, the inside room is open and airy. The tables are spaced nicely, giving everyone lots of room, and the chairs are topped with comfy cushions making any lazy brunch all the more pleasurable. They offer classics like eggs Benedict and the Canadian breakfast (with bacon cured and smoked on the premises, and spicy huevos rancheros or crab cakes and eggs. There is even offer mac'n'cheese and a breakfast burger. For dinner, choose from an ever changing, seasonal menu scattered with pub classics done right.

1378 Notre-Dame ouest
514.931.5249
Metro/Bus: Lucien-l'Allier, or bus 58
Web: griffintowncafe.com
Hours: Tues.: 6:00pm-10pm; Wed.-Fri.: 11:30am-10pm;
Sat.: 10:30am-10pm (brunch until 3pm);
Sun.: 10am-3pm (brunch)
Cards: all major
Wheelchair access: one step
Average meal: $15 (brunch); $25 (dinner)

Grumman '78

It's been a long uphill battle between the city of Montreal and the folks behind the mobile taco truck Grumman '78 who have been struggling to find ways around the city's tight street-food laws. A huge trend across North America, street-food carts and trucks are quickly becoming the next foodie phenomenon, with high-end chefs walking out of the kitchen and getting behind the wheel. Montreal is finally looking to reverse its long-standing rules prohibiting street food. The man behind Montreal's first mobile taco restaurant is chef Marc-André Leclerc, formerly of Au Pied de Cochon and the Liverpool/Joe Beef/McKiernan family. A dream of his, Leclerc found an old fire house emergency vehicle for a good price, gutted it, refitted it with a griddle and hot plate, painted it bright neon green and called it Grumman '78, named after the make and the year of the vehicle. Now with a full catering license and two partners, Grumman '78 is usually seen lurking around Montreal festivals and special events, offering up an ever-changing menu of delicious homemade tacos that are sure to make you an instant fan. The best part about this taco truck? Rain or shine, warm weather or cold, day or night they're out there on the streets, looking for Mexican-food-loving, hungry mouths to feed, and at a great price. To find out where and when this taco truck will magically appear at a venue near you, go to their Facebook page and check it out. Grumman has also opened up a permanent spot in the food court at Le Faubourg, 1616 Ste-Catherine W.

514.290.5125
www.grumman78.com
Cards: cash only
Average price: inexpensive

Hecho en Mexico

Montreal is definitely not known for its Mexican food. Yes, there are places that put meat and cheese into tortillas and drench them in sauce, but that is not authentic Mexican by any means. Mexican is actually one of the most complex cuisines in the world, with a wide range of spices, sauces and techniques that take years to master. Once in a while I discover a truly authentic find, and although Hecho en Mexico (Made in Mexico) is offering a simpler side of Mexican food, this family-run business is doing it right. Situated in Verdun, it has a large inner courtyard *terrasse* with plenty of space between the tables. The chalkboard menu changes often and is written in Spanish, although the printed menu is in Spanish and French. The servers are more than happy to guide you through the choices. With little baskets of homemade tortillas and an unusual salsa brought to your table, an order of their out-of-this-world guacamole is a definite must. The ceviche—morsels of white fish diced and mixed with lime juice, coriander and tomatoes—is also very good and a perfect accompaniment to an ice cold beer on a hot summer night. The meat combinations for mains vary, but the tacos, presented on large serving dishes with the meat and sometimes cheese mixture piled in the center, are simple and satisfying. The tortillas themselves, made in-house, are some of the best I've had in this city. If you're like me and enjoy a genuine food find, Hecho en Mexico is for you.

4816 Wellington, Verdun
514.439.3868
Metro/Bus: de l'Église
Hours: Mon.-Fri.: noon-9pm; Sat.-Sun.; 2pm-10pm
Cards: V, MC, Interac
Wheelchair access: no
Average meal: $16

Ice House

Ice House is the brilliant new restaurant from the team behind one of my all-time Montreal favorites, Kitchenette. The chef/ owner, Nick Hodge, a Texan born and raised, decided that Montreal needed a southern-style restaurant with good Tex-Mex inspired food and a no frills attitude. Taking over a little spot on the corner of Roy East and St-Dominique, this 24-seat restaurant has a front *terrasse* that seats another 24. With a roll-up garage window at both the front and side of this cozy space, this is one of the hottest places to eat in the summer. The menu is chalkboard style and offers some delectable options like Nick's famous tacos—from beef to fried chicken to pork, as well as burritos (try the lobster), buckets of fried chicken and ribs, an amazingly killer oyster po'boy sandwich, and a variety of hard-to-resist sides like the crab-stuffed jalapeños. Also on this fabulous menu are oysters presented Southern style—on top of a soda cracker, with Nick's home-made cocktail sauce and Tabasco. With bourbon, pitchers of beer, and homemade iced tea and lemonade, how can you go wrong? If you're a Caesar drinker, do yourself a favor and try Ice House's take on it—amaziangly good.

51 Roy est
514.439.6691
Metro/Bus: Sherbrooke, or bus 55
Hours: Tues.-Sat.: 5pm-1:30am
Cards: V, MC
Wheelchair access: two steps
Average meal: $18

Il Cortile

One of Montreal's best-kept *terrasses,* Il Cortile offers above-average Italian food in a picturesque, scenic inner courtyard setting. Open for over 30 years, this little Italian spot has always been miles ahead in serving authentic Italian food in an environment that makes you think you've just landed in Italy. Along with the polished food comes matching service so be prepared to have all your senses pampered. It is the perfect spot to dine if you're downtown and since it's right next to the Montreal Museum of Fine Arts, you can plan a whole afternoon around lunch or dinner. The courtyard itself is long and narrow and overlooks the restaurant. From the flowers and awnings right down to the starched linen tablecloths, it's still one of the prettiest outdoor dining settings in the city. It's good to stick with the simple classics here, so try the Caprese salad or grilled seasonal vegetables to start. For mains, check out their Pomodoro sauce for a taste of what a really good, really simple tomato sauce tastes like, go for their lasagna, or try some delicious veal dishes. It's hard to resist an Italian dessert and my personal favorite has always been the tiramisu. Although a little pricey, lunch at Il Cortile is a more affordable way to check it out and see if you want to go back for dinner. I'm sure you'll fall in love with the setting too.

1442 Sherbrooke ouest
514.843.8230
Metro/Bus: Guy-Concordia
Hours: Mon.-Sun.: 11am-11pm
Cards: V, MC
Wheelchair access: yes
Average meal: $35

Jardin de Panos, Le

One of my favorite Montreal BYOB restaurants is also one of my favorite destinations when I want to eat outdoors in the summer. Going strong since the 1970s, Le Jardin de Panos is not breaking any culinary boundaries but instead offers consistently satisfying Greek food with the added bonus of bringing your own bottle. The appropriately painted white and blue façade gives way to a two-storey restaurant with an inner courtyard at the back shaded by foliage and accentuated with flowers and hanging plants to create a comfortable, summery space. It's attractive, spacious, and perfect for lunch or dinner, seven days a week. Sometimes there's a short wait for an outdoor table, but this tends to be the case for most outdoor places in Montreal on a nice summer evening, especially on the very popular Duluth Avenue. The menu offers many of the Greek standards, starting with a Greek salad, fried calamari or the combination cold pikilia platter for sharing, with a little taste of everything (spanakopita, dolmades, tzatziki, eggplant, feta, cucumbers, tomatoes). Mains include my personal pick, the juicy chicken brochette, but also lamb, beef, seafood and moussaka. All come with potatoes and salad, and at about $25-$30 per person, the quality, quantity and atmosphere are worth a visit.

521 Duluth est
514.521.4206
Metro/Bus: Sherbrooke
Web: www.lejardindepanos.com
Hours: noon-11pm daily
Cards: V,MC
Wheelchair access: yes
Average meal: $25

Joe Beef

Five years ago Little Burgundy, an area just south of downtown, was a blip on the restaurant map. With a peppering of antique shops and greasy spoons, it was hardly a Montreal dining destination. Then along came restaurateurs David McMillan, Frederic Morin and Allison Cunningham, who single-handedly lured people from all corners of the city, across the country and around the world to what is now recognized as one of Montreal's best restaurants. The name "Joe Beef" is an homage to Charles "Joe Beef" McKiernan, an Irishman who came to Montreal in the 1860s and opened a tavern where no one was ever refused. A working class hero, Joe Beef was a local philanthropist who was also known for keeping bears in his tavern to restore the peace when things got too rowdy. Joe Beef's backyard *terrasse,* surrounded by their garden where they grow many of the vegetables used in their dishes, is a small oasis in the city. Protected from the summer rain and illuminated with white lights strung across the area, there is no better place to eat outside in Montreal. With an ever-changing, seasonal menu and a phenomenal wine list, the Joe Beef dining experience, from foie gras to oysters, is definitely something special. On the other hand, prices are bit steep, but it's well worth the splurge.

2491 Notre-Dame ouest
514.935.6504
Metro/Bus: Lionel-Groulx
Web: www.joebeef.ca
Hours: Tues.-Sat.: 6:30pm-9:30pm
Cards: all major
Wheelchair access: no
Average meal: $50

Lafleur

No, this is not a mistake. I am actually including this infamous Quebec restaurant chain in this *terrasse* book and I will convince you—if you're not already aware of how good it is—why this is a terrific outdoor dining spot and one that is quintessentially Montreal. First of all, the branch I am writing about is on the side of Highway 20 in Ville St-Pierre. I have fond childhood memories of this Lafleur's, and on a recent visit, to ensure the consistency of quality, I was not disappointed. Definitely the least scenic *terrasse* of the lot, there is something to be said about sitting on picnic tables among the trucks, traffic and a giant overpass, that make this place irresistibly charming. There is not much to it, maybe a dozen or so stools and a narrow counter for a quick meal. Most people take this food to go, or to eat in their cars in the massive parking lot, much like a steamed hot dog tailgate party, minus the party. But surrounding this green and yellow building that has not changed much in the past 30 years are a scattering of picnic tables and benches, just waiting to be filled with eager diners who, like many of us, get that hot dog itch every once in a while. The food is better than you might imagine, with an array of greasy spoon treats including some of the best steamies around, burgers, fries, poutines, and even veggie dogs. From the hike to get here to the drone of the highway across the street, to the packed parking lot of Lafleur devotees, this is one *terrasse* unlike any other in Montreal. Oh, and your meal will cost you under $5. What a steal!

475 St-Jacques ouest (near Gowans Avenue, Ville St-Pierre)
514.364.4324
Metro/Bus: Go by car
Web: www.restaurantlafleur.com
Cards: cash only
Wheelchair access: yes
Average meal: cheap!

Leméac

There are some restaurants in this city that have a certain atmosphere, a mood about them that just makes you want to be there. Leméac, a long-standing Outremont icon, is a favorite among those in the hospitality industry, not only because of its extensive wine list, but also because of the late hours and after-10 p.m. menu offering an entrée and main course for $22. With its long bar lined with seats, black and white tiled floors, bustling French bistro atmosphere, and attractive crowds, Leméac also has a covered terrace that overlooks a quiet residential street. What's great about dining outside at this restaurant is that when the weather is cool in the fall and early spring, they have heat lamps to keep the diners nice and toasty. Some entrées that I like to order are the potted rillettes served with crispy baguette, the vegetable and cheese tian, and the house smoked salmon. For mains, you can never go wrong with their hanger steak served with delicious thin fries, or the braised beef rib with barley. For something on the lighter side, try the salmon tartare with truffle oil or the roasted black cod. For a sophisticated outdoor dining experience, try the superb weekend brunch.

1045 Laurier ouest
514.270.0999
Metro/Bus: bus 80
Web: www.restaurantlemeac.com
Hours: Mon.-Fri.: 11:30am-midnight;
Sat.-Sun.: 10am-midnight
Cards: all major
Wheelchair access: yes
Average meal: $45

Local, Le

Le Local is a stunning dining experience perfectly set in the western edge of Old Montreal. With chef Charles-Emmanuel Pariseau at the helm, Le Local serves contemporary food in a sleek, stylish setting that makes you want to dress up to blend in with the décor. With a large eating area out front beneath a canvas tent, if you're out to impress, this is the place to go. If you're a wine aficionado, noted sommelier Élyse Lambert can pilot you through their wine list and help you choose the perfect bottle for your meal. The menu pays close attention to detail and the dishes offer a complex variety of flavors and seasonal Quebec produce. From the vine tomato gazpacho and blue crab roll to the herb bread-crumbed savory snail cromesqui, grilled red pepper aïoli, crispy fennel, tomato, olives and Niçoise salad, there are many interesting choices for starters. Mains include some twists on Quebec classics like the BLT, homemade porchetta, confit tomato, poutine, or for a bigger appetite, the 12-ounce Portuguese style "AAA" beef strip loin, topped with sunny-side-up duck egg, with a deconstructed oven-baked potato and grilled asparagus. For fish lovers, try the roasted walleye, fennel purée with Pastis, red raisin, soy bean, celery, parsley and prosciutto chip salad or the Atlantic halibut, celeriac purée, grilled asparagus, grapefruit, watercress and caper beurre noisette. Deserts are also good here, and perfect to finish off the meal with a nice espresso. Although the meal itself is not overly expensive, along with a bottle of wine you might want to reserve this restaurant for a special occasion.

740 William
514.397.7737
Metro/Bus: Square Victoria, then bus 61
Web: www.resto-lelocal.com
Hours: Mon.-Fri.: 11:30am-midnight;
Sat-Sun.: 5:30pm.-midnight;
Cards: all major
Wheelchair access: yes
Average main: $40-$50

Magnan Restaurant & Tavern

Magnan, once a working class haven and roast beef mecca, has undergone a few changes since opening up on St-Patrick Street in Pointe St-Charles in 1932. For starters, they let women in the tavern section of the restaurant in the 1980s. They've also expanded, with a Magnan Express for meat purchases and take out, a large dining room in the basement, a more casual eating area upstairs, and an immense summer *terrasse* in the parking lot across the street from the Lachine canal. If you're going to eat roast beef in this city, this is really where you go. And if you're a sports fan *and* a roast beef lover, you've pretty much hit the jackpot. Did I mention you can even sit outside AND watch sports? Although there were whisperings that Magnan's quality had slipped over the years, on a recent visit with family and friends to help evaluate, they all concurred that it was still as good as ever, at least on the meat front. The prices have naturally crept up along the way, but it's still a great place to sit outside and eat a hunk of meat. For Lobster-Fest, it's also nice to enjoy both hot and cold lobster dishes during this summer season special. For Meat lover, sports fan, seafood craver alike, Magnan is a Montreal institution.

2602 St-Patrick
514.935.9647
Metro/Bus: Charlevoix
Web: www.magnanresto.com
Hours: 11am-11pm daily
Cards: all
Wheelchair access: yes
Average meal: $45

Monkland Tavern and Tavern on the Square

Now both well established as go-to spots in their respective neighborhoods, both the Monkland Tavern in NDG and the Tavern on the Square in Westmount have fabulous outdoor dining areas for lunch and dinner in the summer. The original restaurant, the Monkland Tavern is smaller and more intimate, with no reservations and the occasional wait for a table. Their *terrasse* is on the street front and is primed for people watching along the bustling Monkland Village strip. The Tavern on the Square, a more recent expansion, is more spacious, with an outdoor patio on the south-east corner of Westmount square, surrounded by flowers and plants, and shaded by canvas umbrellas. Twice the size of Monkland's terrace, the Tavern's is also usually packed with locals all summer long. The menu, although not the same at both, offers French influenced, bistro fare that ranges from a hearty burger to fish, steaks, and daily specials. There is also great wine lists at both that offer hand-picked selections of private imports, not to mention some fabulous cocktails to sip in the sun. The prices at both spots are moderate, but can get a bit steep depending on your taste in wines.

5555 Monkland Monkland Taverne
514.486.5768
Metro/Bus: Villa Maria
Hours: Mon.-Fri.: 11:30am-11pm; Sat.-Sun.: 6pm-11pm
Cards: all major
Wheelchair access: yes
Average price: $20

1 Westmount Square Tavern on the Square
514.989.9779
Metro/Bus: Atwater
Hours: Mon.-Fri.: 11:30am-3pm;
Mon.-Sat.: 6pm-11pm
Cards: all major
Wheelchair access: Ste-Catherine street entrance to Westmount Square
Average meal: $25

Muvbox: The Lobster Box

Muvbox is one of the most innovative and striking restaurant concepts in Montreal. Built out of an old Maritime shipping container, Muvbox is a self-contained, sustainable structure that folds out into a restaurant, right on the edge of the port in Old Montreal. This location is the very first Muvbox and the invention of Daniel Noiseux, a Montreal restaurateur and entrepreneur who started the Pizzaiolle restaurants in 1981. This particular Muvbox is called The Lobster Box and incorporates solar powered batteries, recyclable materials and biodegradable packaging. Noiseux doesn't want to stop there, with each generation of Muvbox more environmentally friendly than the next. Because this self-contained restaurant is basically outside, it only appears in the summer and offers some of the best of what Quebec has to offer. The small but delicious menu includes clam chowder, lobster rolls sourced from Iles-de-la-Madeleine lobsters, and three pizzas: Margarita, lobster and Brome Lake duck. There is also a selection of ice cream from the Montreal company, Bilboquet. You can sit and eat on one of their stools, or you can take your food "to go" and sit on the grass overlooking the water. Although Montreal has not caught on to the street food trend yet because of antiquated regulations that will soon change, this Lobster Box, for the time being, is as close to street food we're going to get.

360 de la Commune ouest (by the canal)
Metro/Bus: Square Victoria
Web: www.muvboxconcept.com
Hours: 11:30am-9pm daily—during summer,
weather permitting
Cards: cash only
Wheelchair access: yes
Average meal: $15

Omma

Omma means mom in Korean and that's just the kind of food that is served here—inspired by the chef and owner Mikyum Kim's home cooking. Taking over the spot on the corner of Bernard and Esplanade where the Brazilian restaurant Senzala used to be, there is a great *terrasse* that lets you take in all the sights and sounds of this vibrant Mile End neighborhood while enjoying authentic Korean cuisine. With waitresses wearing cute floral aprons and Kim in the kitchen running the show, there are plenty of interesting dishes even for those unfamiliar with Korean food. Take your pick to start with choices ranging from Korean dumplings—steamed or fried with either beef or vegetables, chicken wings, fried squid or even their Korean pancake. For mains you can play it safe with BBQ chicken or beef ribs served on a hot plate with kimchi, rice, romaine and sesame leaves to make little wraps, or you can go for the classic Korean dish bibimbap. Served in a hot stone bowl, this dish is composed of rice, kimchi, pickled vegetables, sprouts, carrots, red chili paste with a fried egg on top. Although they do play it a bit on the safer side of spice here, you can always ask for more chilies with your meal. With a sweet staff on hand to help and some solid dishes, there is nothing better to complement a little summer heat than some spicy Korean at Omma.

177 Bernard West
514-274-1464
Mon-Sun: 6-11pm; Sat & Sun brunch 11am-3pm
Credit cards: all major
Wheelchair access: one step inside
Average meal: $25

Paris-Beurre, Le

There are some great *terrasses* on Van Horne Avenue in Outremont, but one of the nicest has to be in the backyard at the French bistro, Le Paris-Beurre. A favorite among those who live in the area, this hidden patio is festooned with plants, flowers and even grape vines. It's quietly tucked in amongst residential buildings and houses and can seat up to 60 people. Spacious, calm and with candlelit tables, Le Paris-Beurre is also a great place to go on a date. If you live too far away to stroll over, an added bonus is that there is a parking lot for customers—a rarity in this part of town. With a menu of typical bistro fare and added seasonal touches, Le Paris-Beurre's owner and chef, Hubert Streicher, has been there since he opened the place in 1985. The menu highlights a range of French classics including veal, duck and fish. There is also a daily table d'hôte with specials that include your choice of entrée, main and coffee. Some of my favorite starters include the chicken liver mousse served with a red onion compote or the very simple asparagus in a balsamic vinaigrette. For mains, I like to go with the crispy-skinned grilled duck breast, or a French fish staple, skate wing with capers and lemon. The wine list offers a wide selection of both Old and New World bottles, with a couple of nice choices under the $40 mark. Le Paris-Beurre's *terrasse* is a hidden gem—perfect for a very French night out.

1226 Van Horne
514.271.7502
Metro/Bus: Outremont
Web: www.leparisbeure.com
Hours: Mon.-Fri.: 11:30am-2:30pm, 5:30pm-10pm
Cards: V, MC
Wheelchair access: yes
Average main: $28

Pasta Casareccia

There is something so satisfying about finding a good Italian restaurant—one with simple dishes, homemade pastas, and reliability that keeps you coming back for more. I've been eating at Pasta Casareccia since I was fifteen-years-old, and I still make my way to NDG every time I get a craving for their penne arrabiata. Located on Sherbrooke Street, Casareccia has not changed much over the years, which is partly why I love it so much. They recently expanded to include a new room at the back, but the bright red banquette and yellow painted walls remain loudly intact. In the summer, they erect a small terrasse on the street front for some *al fresco* dining. They sell quality imported Italian products such as oils and vinegars, olives, tuna and preserves. They also package their sauces and sell fresh pasta along with most of the items on the menu over the counter. The restaurant's menu is pretty simple with a small selection of salads and antipasti to start, and then a mix and match of pastas and sauces that you can combine to your liking. A family-run affair, Pasta Casareccia is casual and comfortable and always a perfect choice when you get a craving for pasta.

5849 Sherbrooke west
514.483.1588
Metro/Bus: Vendome then 105 bus
Web: www.pastacasa.ca
Hours: Mon.-Wed.: 10am-9pm;
Thurs.-Sat: 10am-10pm; Sun.: 11am-9pm
Cards: all major
Wheelchair access: yes
Average meal: $30

Petit Alep, Le

When choosing a restaurant, diversity is one thing Montreal truly has in its favor. Le Petit Alep offers Syrian cuisine in a relaxed, family-style atmosphere. Located right next door to their more formal dining room, Alep, I prefer Le Petit for its very affordable prices. With two separate outdoor eating areas to the left and right of the entranceway, you'll find yourself dining right across the street from the bustling Jean-Talon Market. A good way to start this meal is by sharing a variety of their dips and salads, served with charming little baskets filled with bags of mini pita bread. Try the fattouche salad, the hummous or the muhammara, a walnut garlic spread with pomegranate molasses. For mains, there are several meat options, either served wrapped in a pita, or with rice and salad. The chicken and lamb are excellent, but my pick is the tender spicy morsels of filet mignon for an incredible $11. The variety of the wine list is worth noting, and is available by the glass, half-glass and half-bottle. Le Petit Alep does not take reservations, but even if you have to contend with a short wait, it's definitely worth it!

191 Jean-Talon east
514.270.9361
Metro/Bus: Jean-Talon
Hours: Tues.-Sat.: 11am-11pm
Cards: V, MC, Interac
Wheelchair access: yes
Average meal: $18

Philinos

Montreal has an abundance of Greek restaurants that span all budgets and dining tastes. Along Parc Avenue, there are some of this city's best spots, but for a unique outdoor experience, Philinos is a great bet. Located just above Mount-Royal, Philinos' leafy trellised patio just outside the entrance of the restaurant manages to spirit you away from Parc's busy chaos. Shaded from the sun and protected from the street, it's the perfect place to enjoy an authentic Greek meal. With an emphasis on seafood, the menu has a variety of hot and cold entrées, dishes for sharing and nice cuts of meat. You can never go wrong with a little fried calamari or grilled octopus accompanied, as always with creamy tzatziki and maybe a little spanakopita on the side. All main courses come with your choice of soup or salad, but the Greek salad is always fresh and satisfying. Choices include lamb chops, grilled shrimp, and a selection of combination platters, even vegetarian moussaka. If you're into wine, Philinos offers some interesting Greek varietals which they will be happy to recommend and let you taste. Eating at Philinos is always a convivial experience, however, it's usually packed so be sure to make a reservation.

4806 Parc
514.271.9099
Metro/Bus: Laurier then bus 51; or bus 80
Web: www.philinos.com
Hours: Mon.-Thurs.: noon-11pm;
Fri.-Sat.: noon-midnight; Sun.: noon-11pm
Cards: all major, Interac
Wheelchair access: yes
Average meal: $30

Pho Tay Ho

Nothing beats a traditional Vietnamese pho soup and Pho Tay Ho offers one of the best in the city. Located in a narrow spot on St-Denis just below Beaubien, not only is the food delicious and cheap, they have both a front and back *terrasse* for summer dining. Although located on a busy street, it's very residential and the atmosphere, while sitting under their covered patio overlooking the neighborhood, is unsurpassed. As soon as you take your seat, you are offered a pot of complimentary tea. The menu is quite elaborate with plenty of vegetarian and non-vegetarian choices, but the pho here is really where it's at. Pho is a rich, complex broth served with your choice of meat (or combination of meats), noodles, fresh basil, sprouts, chillies and lime. It's then up to you to add hot sauce, hoisin, fish sauce or even soy sauce to your liking. (There is nothing that cools you down better on a hot summer day than a bowl of spicy soup.) My favorite is the simple pho with slices of rare beef that cook in the hot broth when it's served. If soup doesn't appeal to you, there are plenty of pork dishes, salads, chicken and vegetables. If you are a fan of Vietnamese cuisine, Pho Tay Ho is right up your alley.

6414 St-Denis
514.273.5627
Metro/Bus: Beaubien
Hours: 10am-9pm daily
Cards: Interac
Wheelchair access: yes
Average meal: $15

Pizzeria Napoletana

When it comes to thin, crispy, authentic pizza pies, I can't get enough, especially with a salad and a refreshing glass of white wine on a hot summer night. Unfortunately, this is one thing that is lacking in Montreal; a big surprise considering the abundance of Italians and Italian restaurants. If anyone ever asks me where to go for a good pizza, I usually recommend Pizzeria Napoletana in Little Italy. If you're looking for a quiet meal where you can have an intimate conversation, unless you're outside on the street front tables or on the side *terrasse*, I would recommend take-out. Inside, it's bright, busy and full of echoing banter emanating from the adjoining dining rooms. That being said, the pizza here is wonderful, the atmosphere is a lot of fun, and the outdoor seating areas make for a perfect, inexpensive dinner out, especially with the bonus that you can bring your own wine. Open since 1948, Napoletana claim they were the first in the city to make traditional-style pizzas. With their original wood-burning oven, these pies come out pretty fast and one pizza is perfect to share between two people, depending on your appetite. I like simple pizzas, so my pick is usually the buffalo mozzarella with tomato and fresh basil, but there are plenty of choices, from vegetarian, to meat and seafood. They also have pasta dishes and they serve excellent coffee.

189 Dante
514.276.8226
Metro/Bus: Jean-Talon; or 55 bus
Web: info@napoletna.com
Hours: 11am-11pm daily
Cards: cash only
Wheelchair access: 2 steps
Average meal: $18

Rumi and Rumi Grill & Café

Rumi, named after the 13th-century Sufi poet, is an enchanting restaurant serving quality Middle Eastern cuisine in the Outremont-Mile End neighborhood. Equally good, but more casual and affordable, is their offshoot Rumi Grill and Café. The original restaurant has a more sheltered, peaceful *terrasse* out front, with red awnings, wood accents and plants, located on a quiet corner just off Parc Avenue. Rumi Grill and Café is on busy St-Laurent Boulevard and the outdoor tables are on a little cordoned off area out front on the sidewalk. Both specialize in authentic dishes. A ideal way to start the meal at Rumi is to share a selection of their hot and cold entrées, including hummus, labneh, babaganoush, merguez sausage or fresh salads. For mains, try any tagine dish or the oven-baked salmon with a tamari, maple syrup and ginger sauce. You have to taste the falafels at Rumi Grill and the grilled meats served with rice and salad, or pita sandwiches topped with pickles, tomatoes, parsley and sauce. There are platters to share, and delicious grilled vegetarian options. Although the Rumi experience is a more sit-down affair, Rumi Grill is a great way to get a taste of this amazing food when you're on a budget.

4403 St-Laurent Rumi Grill
514.670.6770
Metro/Bus: Mont Royal; or 55 bus
Web: www.rumigrill.ca
Hours: Mon.-Wed.: 11:30am-9pm; Thurs.-Sat.: 11:30am-10pm; Sun.: 10:30am-9pm
Cards: all major, Interac
Wheelchair access: yes
Average meal: $15

5198 Hutchison Rumi
514.490-1999
Metro/Bus: Mont-Royal, then 97 bus
Web: www.rumigrill.ca
Hours: Mon.-Thurs: 5pm-10pm; Fri.-Sat.: 11am-11pm; Sun.: 11am-10pm.
Cards: all major
Wheelchair access: Yes
Average meal: $25

Santropol

The story behind this Montreal café is a genuine labour of love. As soon as you enter their fabulous *terrasse*, you can see why Santropol holds a special place in many Montrealers' hearts. Garth Gilker, the man who started it didn't actually want to open a restaurant at all; he wanted to stop a block of buildings on St-Urbain Street from being demolished in the 1970s. Realizing that it would be harder for the city to tear something down if there was actually something there, he cleared out the space, painted it, and decided, because there was no kitchen and city regulations against cooking, with the exception of boiling water, to open a soup and sandwich café. With very few alternative cafés in the city at that time, and Santropol's proximity to several universities, the idea slowly caught on. About a year after opening, James Solkin and Jennifer Luczynski joined Gilker and have been partners since. The garden in the back is truly special, and a pleasure to eat in. Sitting among flowers, plants, trees and a fishpond, this area, filled with nooks and crannies (and the occasional cat), can accommodate up to 30 people. Heaters are set up when it gets cool so patrons can still enjoy the atmosphere and the sun. The menu has an extensive selection of salads and sandwiches and is a good choice for vegetarians. Although not licensed for alcohol, there are plenty of juices and teas to choose from. Often touted as one of Montreal's best *terrasses*, Santropol's history and eclectic setting can't be beat.

3990 St-Urbain
514.842.3110
Metro/Bus: Sherbrooke then bus 144, or bus 55
Web: www.santropol.ca
Hours: 9am-midnight daily during summer
Cards: all major, Interac
Wheelchair access: yes, through the garden
Average meal: $12

Satay Brothers

Inspired by both their mother and their Singaporean roots, brothers Alex and Mat Winnicki are bringing a little East Asian spice to the Atwater market. What started as a few open air food stalls last year has now grown to a full outdoor summer food court with music, picnic tables with St-Henri boys Alex and Mat's infamous Satay Brothers front and center. Using local, seasonal produce and meat sourced on site, there could be no better place to do some shopping, sit down and relax with some amazing food. Serving up a variety of their namesake satays, like chicken and shrimp, they also do a pretty mean steamed pork bun. Mouthwatering pieces of braised pork are wrapped in a soft fluffy rice flour bun with cucumber, spring onions and cilantro. On the lighter side there's a green papaya salad, the perfect refresher on a hot summer day. My all time favorite is sitting down with a big bowl of laksa—a coconut, curry and broth concoction with noodles and seafood or meat. Absolute bliss. The Satay Brothers have specials every day and their menu always changes so you just have to go down there and take a chance—it's totally worth it!

Atwater Market
138 Atwater Avenue
514.661.6983
Metro/Bus: Lionel-Groulx
Hours: Thurs-Mon: 9am-6pm; closed Tues.;
Thurs. & Fri.: 9am-7; Sat. & Sun.: 9am-5pm.
Cards: cash only
Wheelchair access: yes
Price range: $2.50-$8

Tachido

Mexican food has always been hit or miss in this city; unfortunately with a lot more misses than hits. In the past few years though, Mexican has been getting a makeover and places are now popping up serving food reflecting the genuine cuisines of Mexico. One such place is a sliver of a restaurant on busy Parc Avenue between Bernard and St-Viateur. There has been a culinary revival on a somewhat desolate strip mostly known to locals. Tachido is just what the neighborhood needs. Slang for "it's cool" Tachido is a family-run business made up of Mariano Franco and his parents. With Mexican-style street food inspired by the Zócalo district in Mexico City, the menu is simple, but the food is good. With linoleum-topped tables and plastic chairs, there are only about 20 seats inside, but when the weather warms up they set up a half-dozen tables out front on the sidewalk. Open for lunch and dinner, this is the ideal place to sample their wonderful tortas—a Mexican sandwich—on their homemade bread (with a gluten-free option). With fillings ranging from pork, chicken, tofu, and even ham and pineapple, theses hearty sandwiches are packed with flavor. They also have a variety of quesadillas on homemade corn tortillas and these are not to be missed. My favorite is the chicken, served with onions and cheese and dipped in their own hot sauce, either chipotle or jalapeño. Their desserts—a pineapple jam cake made by Franco's mother, or scones with almonds made by his father—tend to sell out pretty fast so you might want to get there early. Sunshine, a beer and some Mexican food are all you really want on a hot summer day; so play it cool and pop by Tachido for a taste of Mexican street food.

5611 Parc
514-439-0935
Metro/Bus: Place-des-arts, then 80 or 435 bus
Tue-Fri: 11am-8pm, Sat: 12-9pm, Sun: 12-6pm
Cards: all
Wheelchair access: no
Average meal: $10

Tripolis

Sometimes, through word of mouth, you stumble upon a gem of a restaurant that you would never never normally looked at twice had you walked by. This is the case with Tripolis situated in the heart of Park Extension, on a busy little strip in a residential neighborhood. The sounds of Greece are in the air when you walk into this restaurant—you don't feel like you're in Montreal anymore. Tripolis is small and bright and slightly gaudy, but the *terrasse* is really where it's at. Slightly elevated and partially sheltered from the street you still get to observe, over the railing of the *terrasse,* the Arab men smoking on their evening stroll, Indian women passing by in their saris, and the Greeks in animated conversation with each other. The staff is friendly and the food is well-priced and delicious. Try their thick and creamy tzatziki to start, with the char grilled octopus salad scattered with onions and capers, and the melt-in-your mouth spanakopita, which arrives in a big square that you divide yourself. It's very easy to share mains and all meals come with a choice of salads—the Greek Village salad being the clear winner. Lamb, pork and chicken are all great and there is also plenty of seafood to choose from. On a hot summer night there is nothing better to complement this great meal than Mythos, the refreshingly light, Greek beer.

679 St-Roch
514.277.4689
Metro/Bus: Parc then bus 80
Web: www.tripolisrestaurant.com
Hours: Sun.-Tues.: 11am-2am;
Fri.-Sat.: 11am-4:30am
Cards: no, but ATM in restaurant
Wheelchair access: no
Average price: $10 for souvlaki, $21 for steak

Voro

The Mile End district is not an area known for its abundance of *terrasses*, partly due to the small restaurant spaces available, and the predominently residential streets. Although there are plenty of places to sit out and drink coffee, eating a good meal outside is its own challenge. A newer restaurant in the area, Voro, the Latin word for "consume", combines French, Italian, Spanish and Middle Eastern cuisines to form an eclectic menu made up of tapas (for a lighter meal), salads and main courses at very reasonable prices. Located in a spacious modern loft on the corner of Fairmont and Jeanne-Mance, Voro has a large outdoor seating area that wraps around the corner of the building and is great for people-watching in this young, hip part of town. With a very reasonable wine list, and open for weekend brunch and daily lunch and dinner, this is a recommended outdoor dining option. Some of the menu highlights are the lamb phyllo tapas served with yoghurt dipping sauce or the stuffed calamari with chorizo and rice. Try the braised beef sandwich for a satis-fying lunch, or for dinner the chicken and preserved lemon tagine. With a team of young talented people behind this new restaurant, and a great *terrasse* to enjoy the summer heat, this is sure to be a very popular neighborhood spot.

275 Fairmont ouest
514.509.1341
Metro/Bus: Laurier then bus 51; or bus 80
Web: www.voro.ca
Hours: Mon.-Wed.: 8am-11pm;
Thurs.-Sat.: 8am-1am; Sun.: 8am-5pm
Cards: V, MC
Wheelchair access: yes
Average main: $15

Neighbourhood Index

Cuisine Index

PLUS OTHER CATEGORIES